| THE **Future Interior Designer's** HANDBOOK | FUTURE INTERIOR DESIGNER: | DATE: | SCALE |
| | PROJECT: | | ¼ INCH = 1 FOOT |

THE
Future
Interior
Designer's
HANDBOOK

Jana Rosenblatt

4880 Lower Valley Road, Atglen, PA 19310

Other Schiffer Books on Related Subjects:
The Future Architect's Handbook, Barbara Beck, ISBN 978-07643-4676-7
The Future Architect's Tool Kit, Barbara Beck, ISBN 978-07643-5193-8

Designed by Justin Wilkinson
Drawings by Jana Rosenblatt
Photography by Lisa Bevis

Type set in Proxima Nova

ISBN: 978-0-7643-6404-4
Printed in India

Published by Schiffer Publishing, Ltd.
4880 Lower Valley Road
Atglen, PA 19310
Phone: (610) 593-1777; Fax: (610) 593-2002
Email: Info@schifferbooks.com
Web: www.schifferbooks.com

For our complete selection of fine books on this and related subjects, please visit our website at www.schifferbooks.com. You may also write for a free catalog.

Schiffer Publishing's titles are available at special discounts for bulk purchases for sales promotions or premiums. Special editions, including personalized covers, corporate imprints, and excerpts, can be created in large quantities for special needs. For more information, contact the publisher.

We are always looking for people to write books on new and related subjects. If you have an idea for a book, please contact us at proposals@schifferbooks.com.

CONTENTS

CHAPTER ONE

INTERIOR DESIGN & INTERIOR DESIGNERS

An interior designer makes lives better!

He or she combines artistic talent with knowledge of building construction and human emotions to create comfortable, functional, and beautiful spaces. After an interior designer's job is done in a home or place of business, people can live and work at their best.

Interior designers are like painters who dip their brushes into many different pots of paint to create a finished piece of art. But instead of just colors, they choose the materials for the walls, floors, and windows. They organize space and decide how a room will function efficiently with its tables, chairs, lamps, and accessories.

How the inside of a building makes you *feel* is an important part of what an interior designer does. Does your own house feel warm and cozy? Do you feel like you can run in the hallway and bounce on the sofa? Or do you feel you need to be on your best behavior? When you walk into a store, does it feel sparkly and fun? How about your doctor's office—is it colorful and welcoming, or a little bit scary?

In this book, we will study the drawings and decisions that Taylor, an interior designer, made to turn the attic of her house into a guest bedroom, bath, and home office.

When Taylor was little, she loved to draw and to rearrange the furniture. At age ten, her parents let her redesign her bedroom. She chose a new bed, desk, and bookcase; a green area rug; and curtain fabric with colorful stripes. Taylor painted the walls yellow and hung a bulletin board and framed photos of her friends.

What do you have on your bedroom walls?
Where do you keep your books and favorite things?
What would you like to change in your room?

In high school, Taylor loved art and design classes so much that she went on to earn a college degree in interior design. Her studies included art, architectural history, kitchen and bathroom design, and how to design with color. She also took classes in business and marketing. In her favorite class she learned how to create computer-generated drawings and building plans.

After college, Taylor worked in an interior design studio with many other talented men and women. They designed the interiors of lots of different kinds of buildings, from houses to hospitals.

Recently, Taylor realized she needed more room in her house and decided to renovate the attic. The floor and walls are unfinished, and it is dark and cold in the winter and hot in the summer. When she opens the door and looks up the stairs, all she can see in the darkness is the clutter of things her family has been storing in the attic for many years. But Taylor has imagined an attractive, useful space.

First Taylor will draw the plan of her attic as it currently exists, so she will know the size and shape of every wall and corner.

Next, she will draw the design plans, showing the changes she would like to make. Let's talk about the changes one by one. But first, we need to understand more about all the things that go into making attractive, functional spaces.

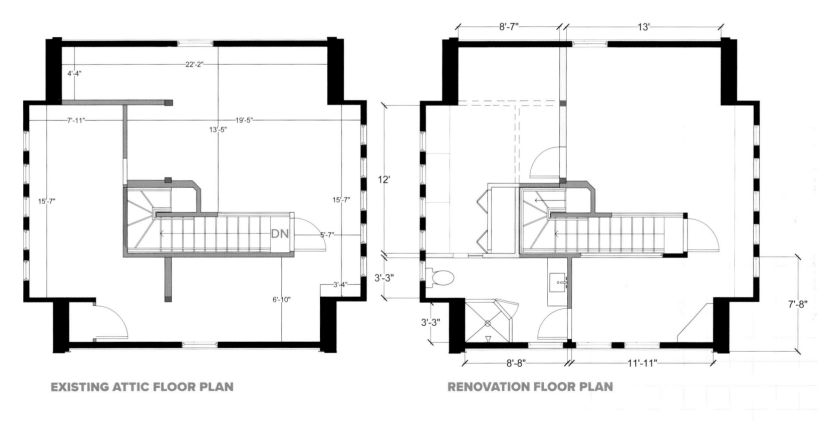

EXISTING ATTIC FLOOR PLAN

RENOVATION FLOOR PLAN

CHAPTER TWO

INTERIOR DESIGN COMPONENTS

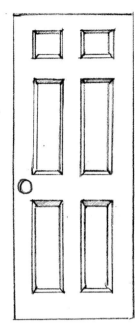

Every building interior is different, yet all rooms share the same basic elements. These are the windows and window coverings, doors, flooring, built-ins, furniture, plumbing fixtures, lighting, and accessories.

There are as many kinds of *windows and doors* as there are kinds of homes and buildings. The door's functions are protection from the elements, privacy, and security. The door's style should enhance the building's architecture.

A door can have many panels, have a single panel, or be flat.

Some doors have louvers or screens that let air flow through.

A barn door rolls on a track.

Double doors that open are called French doors.

Doors that move side to side are called sliding doors.

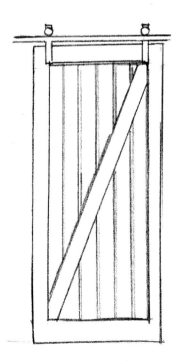

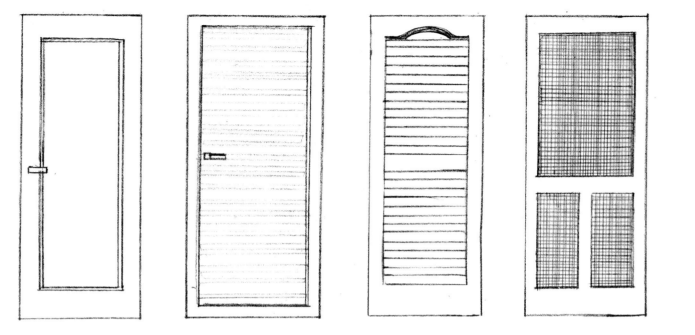

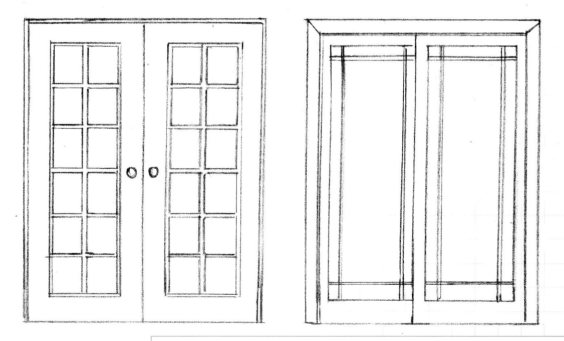

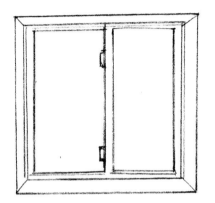

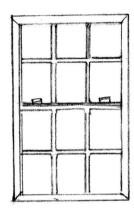

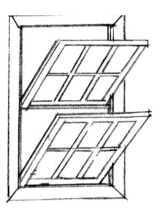

SLIDER

SINGLE-HUNG

DOUBLE-HUNG

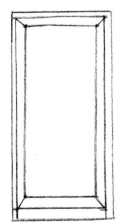

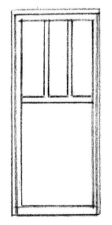

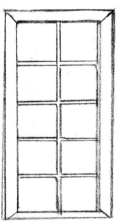

CASEMENT

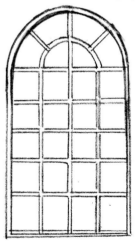

Windows let in natural light, which makes us feel happy, reduces the need for electric lights, and warms a space in winter. The direction a window faces in relation to the sun's movement throughout the day will determine the quality and intensity of the light. Does the sun hit your bedroom windows in the morning, waking you up? Does it come into your kitchen in the late afternoon?

Windows are sometimes solid panes of glass that do not open, called "picture windows" because they frame the outside view. When windows face each other across a room, we benefit from cross-breezes that reduce the need for air-conditioning. Here are a few of the most common window types:

Slider windows can be moved from side to side.

Double-hung windows open both top down and bottom up.

Single-hung windows open from the bottom, and the top glass is fixed in place.

Casement windows have hinges and crank open with a handle.

Window coverings help control light, temperature, and sound.

Solid drapes can hang straight down or be held open with a piece of fabric or metal called a tieback.

Lightweight curtains called sheers offer privacy while letting some light in.

Valances are decorative fabric strips that cover the top of a shade.

Window shades move up and down and offer many options for room darkening and light filtering. They can be made of fabric, natural grasses, wood, or plastics.

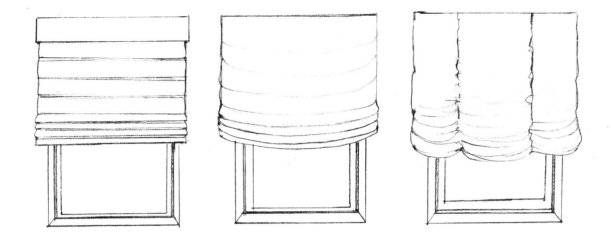

Shutters, wood blinds, and mini-blinds are made of hard materials that can close completely or be adjusted at an angle to filter the sun and breezes.

Solar shades block the sun's ultraviolet rays and heat.

Roman shades can stack above the window.

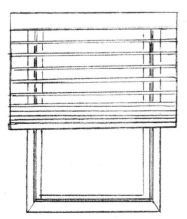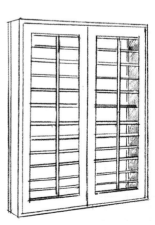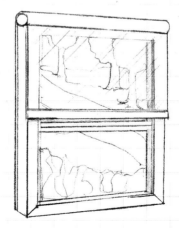

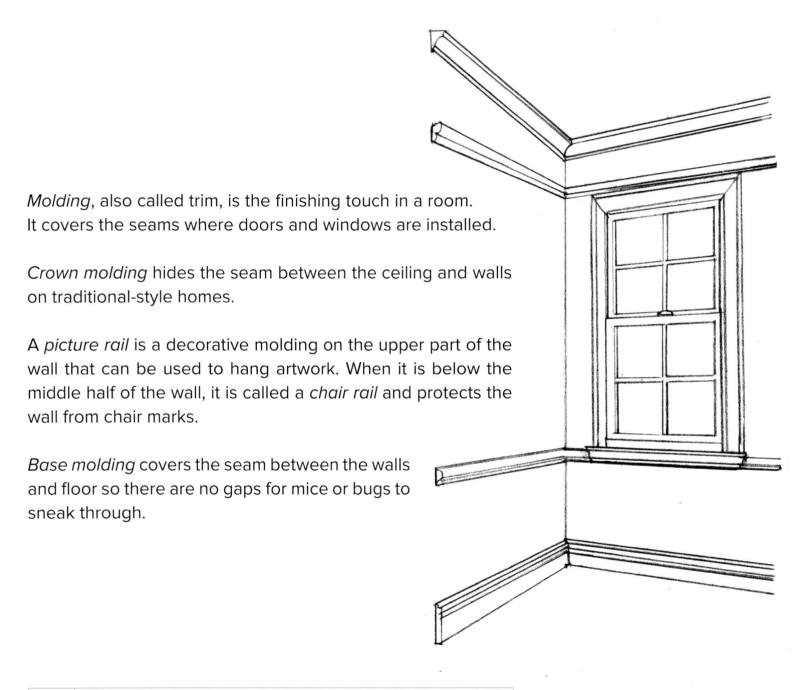

Molding, also called trim, is the finishing touch in a room. It covers the seams where doors and windows are installed.

Crown molding hides the seam between the ceiling and walls on traditional-style homes.

A *picture rail* is a decorative molding on the upper part of the wall that can be used to hang artwork. When it is below the middle half of the wall, it is called a *chair rail* and protects the wall from chair marks.

Base molding covers the seam between the walls and floor so there are no gaps for mice or bugs to sneak through.

Flooring can be made from natural materials like wood planks, stone, or clay tiles. Or, it can be a man-made material such as vinyl, concrete, porcelain, or ceramic. These are the hard surfaces.

Carpet is a soft surface that can be shaggy and thick or flat and tightly woven. It comes in as many colors and patterns as you can imagine.

Properly placed *lighting* is important because it allows us to see clearly at any hour of the day or night. Light can come from lamps that plug into outlets, or from fixtures installed in the ceiling and walls. Different kinds of light fixtures create the mood of a room.

Ambient light is the main light in the room. It can be created with evenly spaced *recessed lights* in the ceiling. Often, ambient light is controlled by a dimmer switch so you can make the light brighter or softer.

Task lighting adds a burst of light in the area where you are working, reading, or cooking. It might be a *pendant light* over your kitchen counter, a *lamp* on the bedside table, a *wall sconce* over the bathroom mirror, or a *floor lamp* next to your favorite reading chair.

Plumbing fixtures are found everywhere that water comes into the house, and they come in many shapes and sizes. These include sinks, faucets, toilets, showers, and tubs. They are made of hard materials such as stainless steel, porcelain, or metals.

The choice and arrangement of *furniture* depends on how the room will be used. In the dining room you will want a table and chairs and maybe a piece for storage and serving food. In the living room you will find a sofa, chairs, coffee table, side table, and maybe bookshelves. The bedroom will have a bed, side table, dresser, and sometimes a chair or desk.

Accessories make a house a home. They are the personal touches: candles, pillows, art, and plants that add personality to a designed space.

BUILT-IN

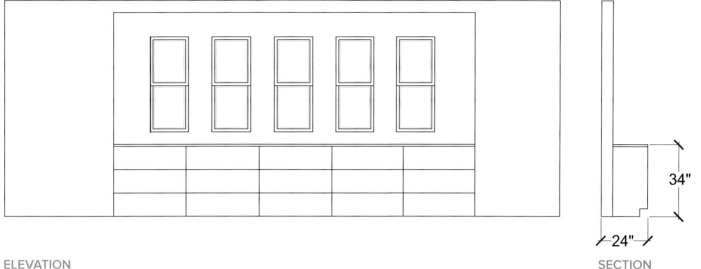

ELEVATION   SECTION

A *built-in* is a cabinet or bench built into the wall. Here is an *Elevation* of the large built-in storage cabinet that Taylor has designed to hold boxes of family photos, holiday decorations, and many things that were stored in the attic. The drawing includes a *Section*, which shows the built-in's height and depth as if you had sliced through the middle of it.

Do you have built-ins in your house?

SCALED DRAWINGS

Architectural drawings communicate Taylor's decisions to the people remodeling the attic. Because you cannot fit a life-size drawing of a room on a piece of paper, you need to shrink it to fit. This is called scale, and it shows how the size of a drawn object relates to its actual size.

Architectural scale is measured in feet and inches. If you imagine that 1 inch on the ruler is equal to 1 foot of a wall length, you are working in *1-inch scale*.

If each ½ inch on the ruler is equal to 1 foot of the wall length, you are working in *½-inch scale*, and so on.

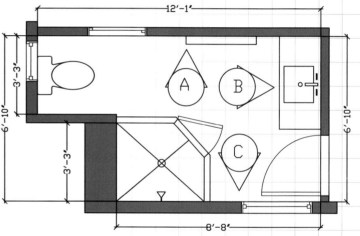

SCALE: ¼"

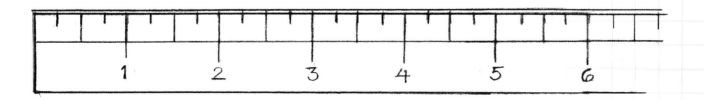

Compare this ½-inch-scale drawing of Taylor's bathroom plan to the ¼-inch-scale drawing on the previous page. Can you see the difference in drawing size?

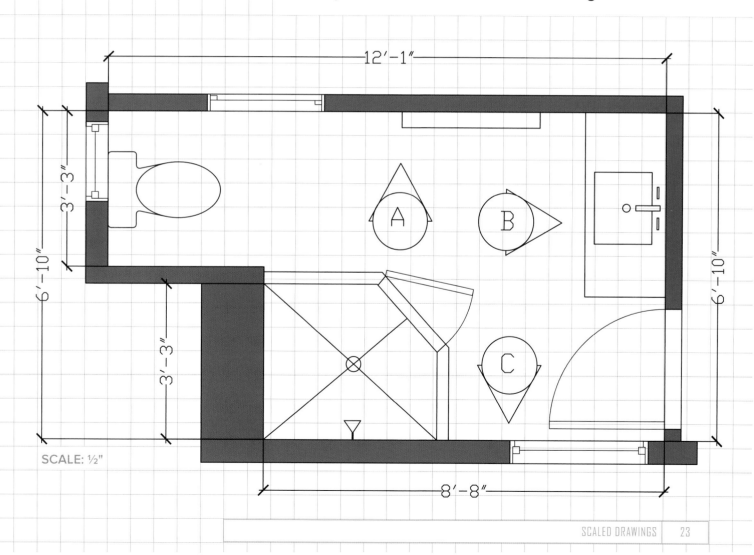

SCALE: ½"

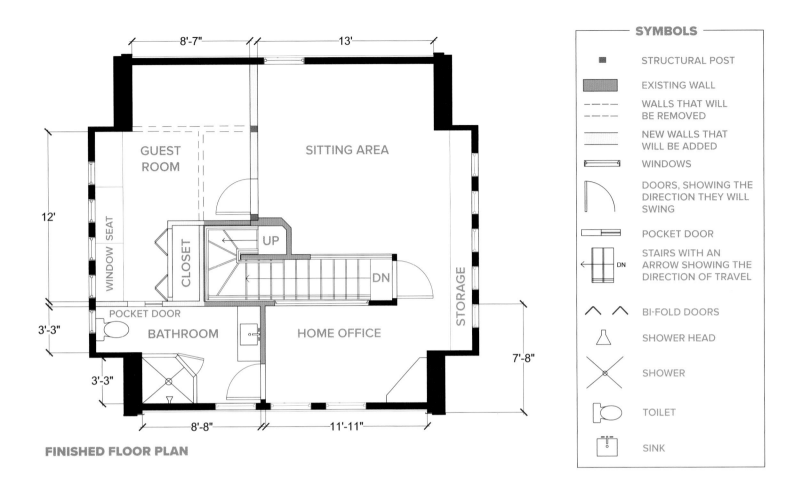

SYMBOLS

■ STRUCTURAL POST

▬ EXISTING WALL

--- --- WALLS THAT WILL
          BE REMOVED

▬ NEW WALLS THAT
      WILL BE ADDED

⊏▭⊐ WINDOWS

DOORS, SHOWING THE
DIRECTION THEY WILL
SWING

⊏▭⊐ POCKET DOOR

STAIRS WITH AN
ARROW SHOWING THE
DIRECTION OF TRAVEL

∧ ∧ BI-FOLD DOORS

△ SHOWER HEAD

✕ SHOWER

TOILET

SINK

FINISHED FLOOR PLAN

A *Floor Plan* is like a road map—a view from above that shows the layout so you can visualize moving through the space. The *Existing Floor Plan* shows what the attic looks like before the changes are made (see page 9). The *Finished Floor Plan* (*above*) shows new walls that will separate the guest room, bathroom, and office, and the location of doors and windows.

Symbols communicate the information on a floor plan without taking up a lot of space.

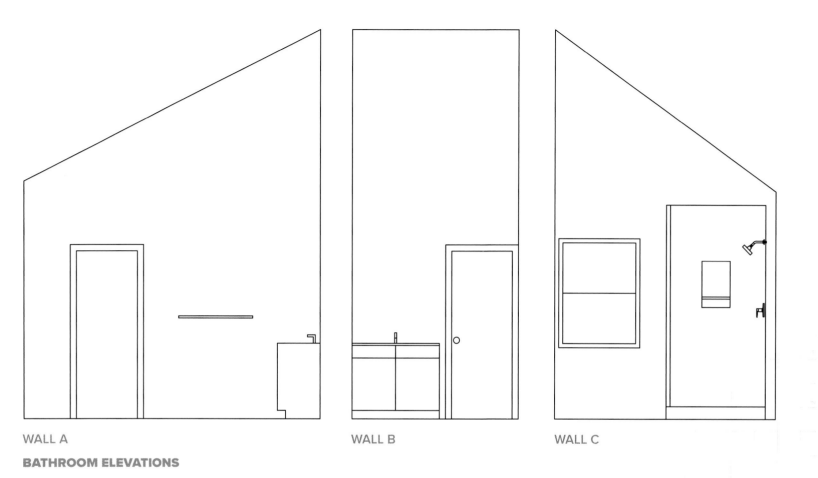

WALL A

WALL B

WALL C

BATHROOM ELEVATIONS

An *Elevation* is a flat view of the three-dimensional details along the walls of a room, including the ceiling, windows, and doors. Usually, ceilings appear as straight lines on the elevation, but in Taylor's attic the ceilings are right under the sloped roof. Together the plan and elevation tell the whole story. They show the place and shape of the selections, such as the closets, built-in cabinetry, and windows.

While Taylor has been drafting the floor plans and elevations, she has been thinking about the furniture and storage space she will need. She will use the floor plan to figure out exactly what will fit. There needs to be enough space around the furniture for people to move around easily. On the *Furniture Plan*, notice the dimensions Taylor has included, indicating the size of each item and the space around them.

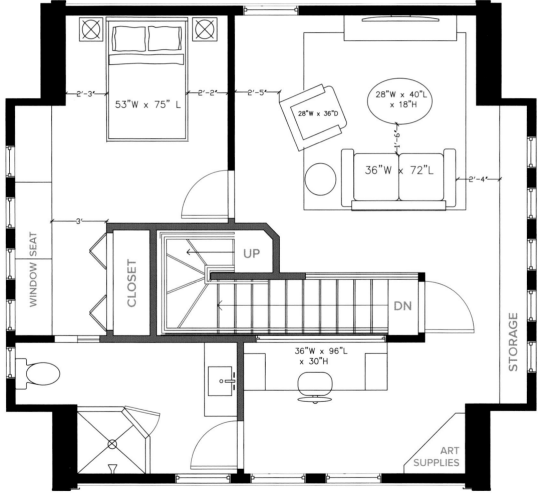

FURNITURE PLAN

CHAPTER FOUR

ARCHITECTURAL STYLE & INTERIOR DESIGN

Taylor works with many different architectural styles. You first notice the style of a home on the outside, and it is the interior designer's job to reflect the building's architectural style on the inside too. This is the basis for her decisions, combined with the personality of her client.

The word *style* relates to many different objects. For example, just as buildings have different styles, so does clothing and furniture.

Traditional-style homes have many variations, but they are all visually balanced and have formal lines. They often have centered entrances with welcoming porches and can be made of brick, stucco, stone, or wood. Inside they have a formal living and dining room on either side of a central hallway, and often a fireplace.

Contemporary-style houses have bold geometric lines, large windows, and an open floor plan. In a contemporary house the furniture might be casual and streamlined, without a lot of frills.

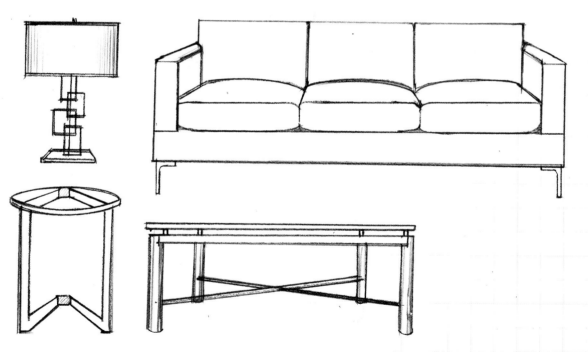

A *transitional-style* house incorporates elements of traditional and contemporary styles. It often has an open floor plan, large windows, and clean, simple shapes.

Taylor's house is country style. This is what it looks like from the outside!

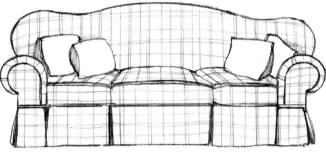

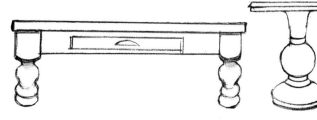

Country-style homes are popular all over the world, with regional details added. You may have heard of French Country, English Country, Southern Country, and even Early American Country. They incorporate elements of nature, with rustic wood or stone and big front porches. Country-style furnishings are usually snuggly and soft with a variety of textures.

There are many more architectural styles, such as Midcentury Modern, Craftsman, Farmhouse, and Cape Cod, to name a few. And there are styles from around the world, such as Spanish, Greek Revival, and English Tudor. There are styles from many eras in history: Colonial, Victorian, Gothic, Italianate, and many more.

One of the primary skills of an interior designer is understanding color! Colors inspire moods and create an atmosphere. Knowing how to select colors, values, tints, tones, and shades is key to creating the mood you want in the spaces you design. To understand color, you need to know a few terms and definitions:

Hue is the word that describes pure color. The three primary colors and three secondary colors on the color wheel are all hues.

The *primary colors* on the wheel are red, blue, and yellow. Because they are not combinations of any other colors, they are the purest *hues*. Pure hues are often used for children's spaces, fast-food restaurants, and places intended to be bright and cheerful. In homes, offices, hotels, and medical facilities, hues are usually toned down to make spaces feel comfortable or soothing.

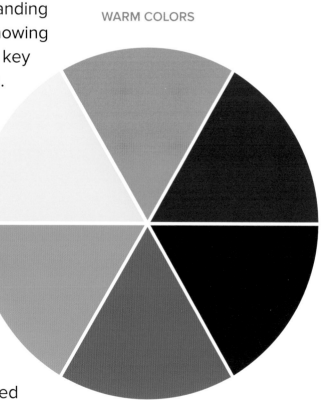

WARM COLORS

COOL COLORS

The *secondary colors* are those created by mixing together the hues on either side of them on the color wheel. They are orange, green, and purple.

Cool colors: Designing with the hues on the cool side of the wheel can make a space feel restful and close to nature.

Warm colors: The hues on the warm side of the wheel make us feel warm, excited, and joyful.

When you mix white, gray, or black to any hue, you get the tints, shades, and tones that create endless palettes to choose from.

Tints are hues mixed with only white and appear lighter.
Shades are hues mixed with only black and appear darker.
Tones are hues mixed with gray, which can have an infinite variety of values and intensity.

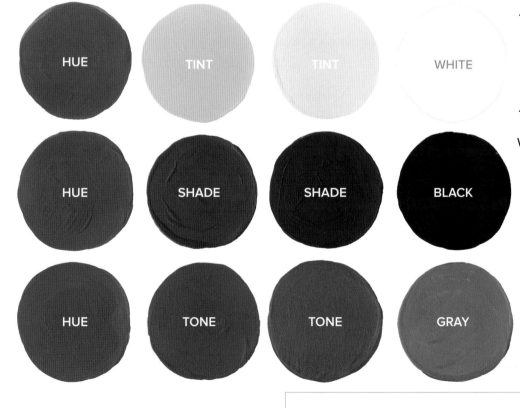

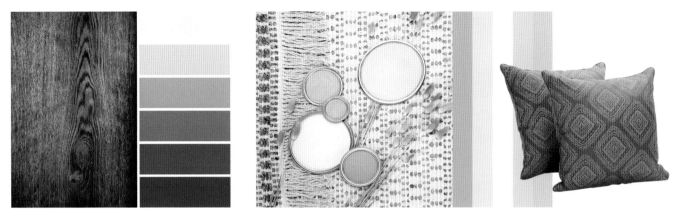

MONOCHRAMATIC   NEUTRAL with hues of gray, beige, and tan   POP of color

Some popular color schemes that interior designers use include the following:

Monochromatic: A single color, with shades and tones of the same color. Often a monochromatic palette is created using colors called neutrals, or earthy browns, greens, grays, beiges, or whites.

Complementary: Two hues that look attractive together. Often they are a combination of warm and cool colors, such as the cool blue of the sea with the warm beige of the sand. Combining a warm color with a cool color in a space creates balance.

Have you ever heard of a *pop of color*? When working with neutral colors in a monochromatic palette, it's fun to spice up the design with a brighter accent color. A turquoise pillow, orange candles, or a multicolored painting can add personality to a room.

The inspiration for a color palette can come from anywhere: a vase of flowers, a painting you love, a photo of a sunset, your favorite sweater—the possibilities are endless, and interior designers must help their clients decide what will most delight and satisfy them.

Complementary color scheme: Orange and blue are opposites on the color wheel.

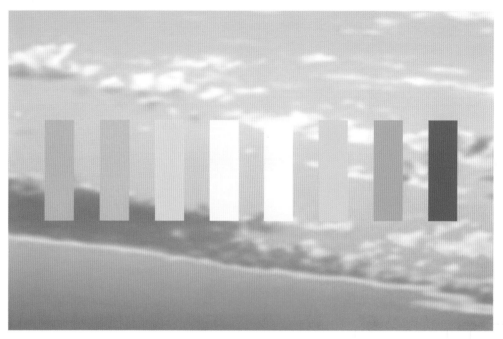

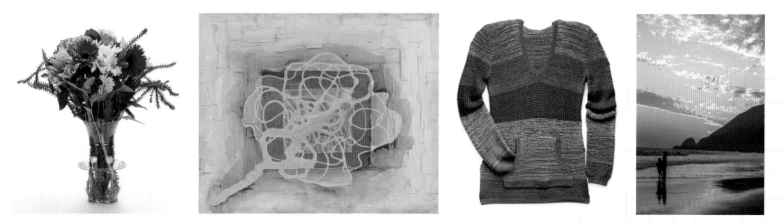

CHAPTER SIX

PUTTING IT ALL TOGETHER

To draw inspiration for her attic project, Taylor thought about the peaceful, relaxed feeling she gets when she walks in the woods with her friends. She wants her guests to feel the same way, and she wants to be inspired by joyful memories when she works at her desk.

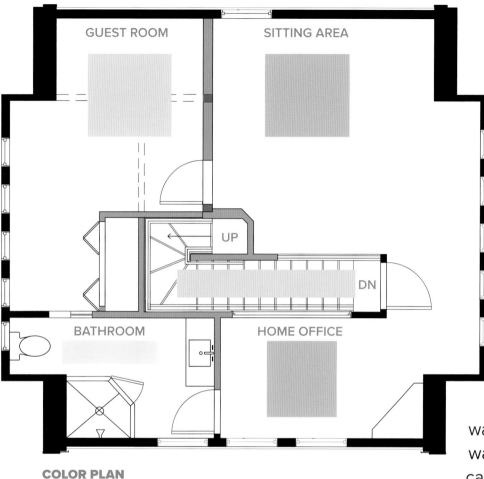

GUEST ROOM

SITTING AREA

UP

DN

BATHROOM

HOME OFFICE

COLOR PLAN

Let's take a look at how Taylor incorporated all of the feelings from her nature walks in the design of her new attic.

First, she identified the blue *hue* that reminds her of the sky and then *tinted* it with white until it was the perfect color for the bathroom walls. This makes the room feel both calm and cheerful.

For the walls in the home office, sitting area, and guest room, Taylor used shades of green that remind her of sunlight filtering through the trees.

To illustrate her color palette, Taylor made a map on top of the floor plan with color samples and notes that a painting contractor will follow.

To communicate her design ideas visually to clients, Taylor makes what is called a *mood board*. It was inspired by her love for nature: warm browns and greens; blue sky and crisp, white clouds; sunlight filtering through trees; and colorful wildflowers.

Mood board for Taylor's attic

The furniture, bedding, and area rugs consist of neutral earth tones. Then she added bright color accents with pillows, throws, and artwork.

Overlapping textures and styles are what make spaces satisfying. Taylor's desk and chair are contemporary, with simple lines and easy-to-clean surfaces, while across the room is a traditional-style sofa with a thick, shaggy rug underneath. The side and coffee tables are wood with curvy details to create a friendly atmosphere.

For the architectural components, Taylor chose windows, doors, and moldings that are historically correct for her hundred-year-old, country-style home (see page 31). The five-panel interior doors match the home's original doors.

She also matched the double-hung windows in the rest of the house; they are split into two equal sections and can open from the bottom up or the top down to control airflow. Her molding selections include a simple window casing and a 4-inch-tall base molding.

The floors in Taylor's home are solid oak. She repeated this in the attic, a reminder of the warm browns of a hiking trail.

Wood flooring is not typically used in bathrooms, because the water and steam can warp it over time. So, she will use porcelain tile close to the color intensity of the wood floor, so the transition will be smooth from room to room. In the shower, Taylor has selected a flooring material made of natural river rocks. The soft, round stones underfoot make you feel like you are showering outdoors. On the shower walls, crisp, white tiles match the style of the house and remind her of clouds. To complete the effect, she painted the bathroom walls a cool, sky blue.

Taylor's plumbing fixtures are shiny, curvy chrome—a good historical choice. Wall sconces on either side of the mirror provide balanced light. White, 2-inch horizontal blinds are a great choice in the bathroom because the blades can be tilted to let in light and breezes while providing the desired amount of privacy.

Taylor has chosen Roman window shades, which make the room dark so guests can sleep late in the morning or take an afternoon nap. They will be made of a textured, striped fabric. A tall mirror leaning against the wall reflects light into the darker part of the room. In the window area where the ceiling is lower, there is a built-in window seat with drawers for extra storage.

The guest room has white-painted, country-style side tables and fluffy bedding with colorful pillows that remind her of wildflowers. There is a closet where guests can hang up their clothes and stash their suitcases. Taylor has allowed 2½ feet of space for people to walk on each side of the bed. An area rug provides comfort and warmth. Over the bed, a carved wood mandala represents the universe and reminds her of tree branches.

In the sitting area and office, which can get hot in the afternoon, Taylor will use solar roll shades. The solar material filters out the sun's harmful rays while allowing light and views to show through the semisheer material.

Taylor placed a small sofa and chair where people can read or watch TV. The TV is mounted on the wall to free up floor space. A table on one side of the sofa can hold a lamp and a drink, and a coffee table is the perfect place to work on a puzzle or stack books.

On the walls she has hung prints by a local photographer and framed pictures of friends and family. Throughout the attic, recessed lights brighten the spaces evenly.

In her office on the other side of the stairs, Taylor placed her desk and computer near the built-in storage containing her art supplies. On the wall is a bulletin board for pinning up important notes and pictures, and beside it is a contemporary painting to inspire Taylor's creativity as she works.

An interior designer's team is made up of many people with different skills and functions. The team could include an architect, a structural engineer, a general contractor, and tradespeople, called subcontractors, such as electricians, plumbers, tile setters, cabinetmakers, and painters. Now that everything is in place, let's review how Taylor's team pulled it all together.

A *carpenter* added interior walls filled with insulation to keep the attic cool in the summer and warm in the winter. After the flooring was installed, a *finish carpenter* installed the base molding and the casing around the doors and windows. An *electrician* looked at Taylor's electrical plan and elevations to see exactly where the wiring for the lighting and electrical outlets will go, and installed the lighting fixtures. A *plumber* installed the pipes that supply water to the new bathroom. When the toilet and sink were delivered, the plumber fastened them into place and added the faucets, spouts, and handles.

The *tile setter* made the shower tile and bathroom floor. A *flooring installer* put down the wood floor. The *cabinetmaker* made the storage cabinets in a shop and then built them into the attic walls. The *painter* used Taylor's color plan to apply the correct paint on the walls. When the furniture was delivered, the movers used the furniture plan to put everything in place. And Taylor added the finishing touches—artwork, pillows, and candles—that give the spaces personality.

It is good to have a college degree and a few years of on-the-job training to become a professional interior designer, but meanwhile you can dream up your own designs. Begin by drawing and playing with colors, textures, and compositions.

Measure a room in your house and draw it to scale on some grid paper. Think about how you can rearrange the furniture. Add the kinds of pieces you need to store things, such as bookshelves, and baskets or boxes with lids. Place artwork or photographs you like on your walls, and selected accessories you love.

Remember, interior design is not just about picking a paint color or sofa, but about space planning and beautifully designed solutions that are personalized for the users. Have fun designing!

ACKNOWLEDGMENTS

My most sincere appreciation to Kim Kuhteubl, author of *Branding + Interior Design,* for connecting me to this wonderful project.

To Lauren Johnson, an accomplished writer and editor, for her instruction and editing, which got me up and going.

To Jessica Kubzansky and Diane Lindley for reading, re-reading, and contributing.

To Larry Kay, Vonnie Walker, Gigi Ushella, Jade Natal, and Luis Dorado for CAD drafting and support.

To Lisa Bevis for the illustrative photos throughout the book, Bonnie Blake for the beautiful sunset photo, and Sara Roizen for the image of her magical painting on page 35.

To Pro-source Wholesale, and Firenze Ceramic Tile, both of North Hollywood, California, for loaning samples and a career of friendship and support.

To Cheryl Weber and Justin Watkinson at Schiffer Publishing for leading me through the process and their creative input.

To my sisters, Amy Farber and Nancy Rosenblatt, and brothers Philip Rosenblatt and Mark Farber, who, along with my mum and dad, fostered and supported my lifelong creative goals!

Most profoundly, thanks to my husband, Tobin Larson, who taught me how to write!

About the | AUTHOR
JANA ROSENBLATT

For Jana Rosenblatt, creating this book was a combination of all her passions—drawing, painting, design, and architecture. Growing up in New England, Jana loved to look at houses for sale with her mother, imagining what she would do with them if she owned them. She loved to draw and design from an early age, which led to her first career as a production and costume designer for film, television, and stage. Her work in the entertainment industry eventually led her back to creating the homes and offices of the people she was working with, and she now runs her own interior design firm, Jana Design Interiors. JDI's projects include new homes, major residential renovations, and office interiors (www.janadesigninteriors.com). She also hosts the podcast *From Disaster to Dream Home*, which helps people think about how to transform the rubble from natural disasters into their dream home. Jana shares her life in Southern California with her husband, Tobin D. Larson, and adopted family Vonnie Walker, Mike Edwards, and twins Alec and Zoey Walker Edwards. For more information, join our community of children who enjoy this book at www.theinteriordesignershandbook.com.

FUTURE INTERIOR DESIGNER:

DATE:

PROJECT:

SCALE

¼ INCH = 1 FOOT